MW00959033

Also by Susan Morgan

The Power of Dreams;
Dream Tools to Navigate Your Life

Death and Continuing On;
A Primer in Interdimensionality

Oracular Divination

Multiple Divination Systems

Susan Morgan

Mystic Dream Publishing House

East Hampstead, NH

Text design: Susan Morgan

ISBN-13: 978-1542623063
ISBN-10:1542623065

This book is dedicated to

My Great Grandmother,

Helen Dufort

and My Grandchildren

Table of Contents

Forward

I owe a debt of gratitude to Robert Moss, who caught me many things including Dreamwork and also how to 'see' better. The Tarot layout that is described in this book, was one that he taught me many years ago and I have taught numerous times to many people since then, always with fantastic results. It is my favorite layout. If I'm in a real big rush I will use a three card layout with the left card being the past, the middle card the present and the right card the future. The ability to read using rocks and sticks and employing a personal Medicine Wheel is a process that was gifted to

9

me by the world of spirit a number of years ago and I thank them. The most important and accurate system of divination is Dreams; the ones that you have every night and that are gifted to you for free. With a little attention to your Dreams, you come to find that many of your Dreams are about the future; or better put *a possible future.*

If it is agreeable, stay on your current course. If it is not agreeable, you will want to change your waking life. Sometimes a small change will re-direct the course, and sometimes a larger change is required. I strongly recommend you learn how to interpret your own Dreams and if you would like to learn how, I teach classes all over the country, offer Online Courses, and am the Founder of the nonprofit **The Mystic Dream Center**, which is dedicated to teaching this ancient and sacred art. I am also the author and my books include, ***The Power of Dreams; Dream Tools for Navigating Life,*** which is also very helpful in explaining how you can easily interpret your own Dreams.

Let's reclaim some of the lost, or often ignored, divination arts, so that we can better direct our own lives toward healing and growth. And to that end, I dedicate this book.

Introduction

When we are able to adjust our sight, we can see things clearer than we do with our everyday eyes and everyday mind. This is more of an art and a skill that most anyone can learn, than some great metaphysical mystery. In ancient days it was primarily the priests and medicine people that used the skills of divination to help their communities. It was not widely taught and maybe in ancient days there was good reason for this. Certainly the people that *were* taught divination skills were the people that had proved themselves to be honorable and possessing integrity. The saying

'Don't Throw Pearls Before Swine' could be applied with this art. If you are Reading or Divining for someone, who is doubtful and cynical of your skill, don't waste your time is my advice.

The art of divination can be used, like most anything else, for the benefit of a group of people or for the empowerment of only one person. I believe if we use divination skills in a manipulative way, then it is more sorcery than anything else. Since I have an understanding of the laws of karma, I go out of my way to avoid anything that even feels like sorcery. I am more concerned about possible kick back, so to speak, on the people I love, like my

14

children and grandchildren, and that prevents me from ever intentionally doing something that could bring harm to anyone else. I know that my life is not perfect, and I am sure I have harmed people in my life, but it is never my intention at this point in my life. Again, not because I am such a holy being, but more because I love people and *don't want to cause harm* to myself or loved ones. It is good advice for any of us.

The Question

> *The Greek word chrêsmologoi, means professional interpreters of oracles.*

When I lead this three-day Workshop, I usually spend at least two hours (!) on the ethics of doing divination work. I discuss the importance of the '*question*' or the inquiry, and how it is the question or the inquiry that is *the most important part of any divination system.* For instance, if the question is, (as it so often is for so many people), "Will I ever find true love?", the great vast Universe will always respond yes. For in the great vastness of your Being, across all time and dimension, you will always find love. It is better to ask, "Is there a strong likelihood for a romantic relationship within the next three months *with my current level of focus on this?*"

This is a better question because it uses the term 'strong likelihood' which is closer to reality than a definite yes or no. Almost nothing is a definite yes or no, and certainly when we change our focus or anything significant in our life, then all the dominoes start falling in a different direction.

Time Frame the Question

I also like to give **time frames** in my question, because that narrows the question to a specific nexus point in time and space and makes the Reading dramatically more accurate. When we ask questions of our Higher Self or the Universe, whichever way you want to look at it, it's always best to put it in a specific time frame. I also like to add the words 'with my current level of focus', or something similar to that, because it *brings responsibility back to the person living their life to help create the life they want* and it also is more accurate with the truth because, again, as soon as we start change our behavior, we end up with a different outcome.

I have done Readings for a number of people who put almost zero effort into a new relationship and yet hope and expect the Universe will deliver their Significant Other to their door. A funny story is there was one woman who specifically expected a man to come to her door since she rarely left her condo. I pointed out to her how crazy that expectation was. She did not think it was crazy and had been married three times. She had a belief system that as soon as men were around her they were inspired to marry her. Since she was in her early eighties when I met her, who was I to argue? But unless you have that unusual background, it is probably safe to say that you're going to have to be involved with more people if you want a new relationship. That does not require psychic skills to come to that conclusion. The actual psychic skills would be the ability to see how much effort any particular person was really putting in their life to finding a new person. Psychic skills are the ability to glean information from a source outside of oneself, or outside of one's normal thinking. It is more of a transpersonal skill then

19

a thinking one. I also discourage people from asking about other people in their Reading, that they really have no business snooping around. Again, this is an ethical approach and you certainly wouldn't want just anyone checking in on you and your personal life psychically.

What I want to teach you has more to do with vision and changing your actual perception of sight so you can look at things with new eyes and get information in ways that you have not been trained to do prior.

Many years ago, I used to say that somebody who could read one thing accurately and authentically, could really read anything.

Cavalierly, I used to say I could read anything

> *Be glad you are not one of the Belly-talkers (engastrimuthoi) that were believed to have gods or demons in their stomachs that prophesied. (see Plutarch, On the Obsolescence of Oracles)*

including rocks, sticks or whatever. I realize for many people they generally only read Tarot for cards, and I used to wonder how this could be. I came to the awareness that there is a way to read Tarot that is more than a scholarly endeavor. If you study the cards and memorize everything then you're able to read them on that level. That is an effective way to read cards.

21

But what I'm talking about is not a scholarly approach at all. You can also learn how to do it very quickly and without years of study. I would also add it is a greater skill than memorization and closer to the level of higher divination use.

You will learn how to look for similarities and differences in the patterns of anything, including the cards, rocks, and sticks. Everything is either coming together, moving apart, or in stasis. What is resonant and what is in discord. Everything is either seen, or unseen.

So if you're ready let's get started!

Chapter One

NEW SIGHT

"I believe in intuitions and inspirations...I sometimes FEEL that I am right. I do not KNOW that I am." Albert Einstein

The first hurdle you're going to have to get over is your relationship with everything. Unless you are indigenous and raised in a culture that taught you things like the four directions, the meanings of color, the elements, and more you are going to have to learn to develop your own personal understanding of these things.

Since I am assuming you don't have access to a shaman for the next ten years to teach you these things, we are going to do a crash course in these right now. And as you deepen your connection with what you are about to learn, it will *continue to grow* throughout your life, which will also increase your ability to work well with many divination systems.

I have found the quickest way to do this is to teach people how to create their own Medicine Wheel. You are not required to be

Medicine wheels, also known as sacred hoops, were constructed by laying stones in a particular pattern on the ground. Most medicine wheels follow the basic pattern of having a center of stone(s), and surrounding that is an outer ring of stones with 'spokes.'

indigenous to have your own Medicine Wheel. The Medicine Wheel that I will help you create will be your own individual wheel that will not look like anyone else's and there's power in that alone.

I would like you to take the time right now to get a large sheet of paper, preferably of high quality. If you don't have any at home, go to a craft or art supply store and get one. If you are able to shamanically journey then you can skip ahead to the next part. I am assuming, that for most of you, you are not familiar with shamanically journeying so I will teach you that skill as well.

Traditionally, the shaman or medicine person was the Healer of a tribal community who could access information in other dimensions. Sometimes it is said they are the Walker Between Two Worlds. The shaman would work with dreams, the departed, and divination; the three D's.

I teach workshops on Dreamwork and am the founder of a non-profit, The Mystic Dream Center, dedicated to teaching the ancient and sacred art of Dreamwork. It is a topic near and dear to my heart. I am also a Medium and can

speak with the Departed. But with the

divination systems that I'm going to teach you,

it could also be understood that you will be a

Walker Between Two Worlds, because you will

be able to access information not normally

understood with your everyday mind. Will that

make you a

shaman? No.

But it *will* allow

The emperor Augustus had more than two thousand oracular books burned to prevent unauthorized access to them.

you the ability to access information in ways

that most people are unaware of. I have taught

thousands of people how to shamanically

journey and I would say 99% of them were

successful in doing so. I am sure you will be as

well.

27

For most people the best way to get into a heightened state of awareness, is to go on a shamanic journey through heartbeat drumming, that just naturally puts us in a relaxed state. At a certain speed of drum beat our brain waves shift and we naturally move from the left side of our brain to the right side of our brain without any intention or striving to do so. It happens easily and naturally. We can go from a Beta state of awareness to a Theta state through this method.

The left side of our brain is a wonderful side and very useful for action, linear thinking, math, amongst other benefits. The right side of our brain is where our creativity and intuition reside and it is sorely under-used by most people.

Problem Solving

But if we want to solve a problem in either our own personal lives or the greater world, *we need Seers*, people that can see beyond the normal. The Seers are working with the *right side* of their brain. Ideally, the best problem solvers are people that use the right side of their brain to come up with the creative idea/solution for a problem and then use the left side of their brain to execute the action required to solve the problem. Again, the right side is the creative idea side, and the left part of our brain is the side that makes it happen. If we primarily work with only our left side then we'll have a tendency of repeating behaviors almost by rote memory. That can also be where addictions and chronic bad behavior reside. If we live too much on the right side of our brain, we will be filled with beautiful ideas and creative inspiration but we will have no practical application for it in our everyday life. We won't be able to accomplish and create the things and situations that we want because we are only producing thought, however creative, but not taking the necessary action.

You may want to ask what does this have to do with divination? Everything. Because I am teaching you a new way to relate to the World at Large. I would like you to practice for a few minutes each day, noticing how much of your day is spent on either the left side or the right side of your brain. As you increase your awareness of which behaviors are coming from each side, try to bring yourself more in balance. If you find most of your day is spent with left brain activity, try to spend some time each day devoted to right brain activity which could be meditating, praying, cooking creatively, singing, dancing etc. I would like you to start *strengthening* the right side of your brain.

There are shamanic drum beats available online, and I also offer that through my website MysticDreamCenter.com. You might find you enjoy shamanic journeying so much that you take up drumming yourself, or you could use a rattle, both are effective. I read somewhere that if we listened to twenty minutes of a shamanic drum beat our white blood cell count goes up. Besides healing for our emotions and our minds, it is also healing for our body.

Practice taking a shamanic journey, one or two times, which typically only last ten minutes or so prior to the next exercises. Do this without feeling any pressure on yourself to accomplish anything. Your intention can be to connect with a guardian in the spirit world. That helper could be a Guardian Angel, an Ancestor, or Spirit Animal, often referred to as totem animal or power animal, in indigenous cultures. When you are in this heightened state of awareness, initially it might feel as if you are making up this 'journey'. I suggest that initially you put all your self-doubt in a basket by the door and let your imagination run free during your initial journeys. You will come to know, by experience, that it is not a fantasy that you are experiencing, but a dimension that is unfamiliar to most people. There are many levels of

33

awareness and also dimensions, but that is not something to concern ourselves with right now. It is enough for us to relax and allow ourselves ten minutes with just our imaginations and a heartfelt intention, to reach out to the world of spirit for a helpful Guardian.

Prayer

I always start with a prayer. I strongly recommend you do the same prior to your journey. Remember, there are all kinds of spirits, good and bad, and when we say a heartfelt prayer to God, for only a true and helpful Guardian to come through for us, we are surrounded and protected by our prayer from chaos and basic trouble making. You will

34

also want to do your shamanic journeys in a quiet place where you'll know you will be undisturbed. You will also want to take notes on anything that you see or feel. It is best to get a journal at this point, to track your journeys, also because this information will be useful in creating your Medicine Wheel and also deepening your awareness of the divination systems I will teach you. After you have done this *at least* two times proceed to the next step.

Chapter Two

MEDICINE WHEEL

"There are two kinds of people in the world: those who are dreamers and those who are being dreamed." Alberto Villoldo

On your (high-quality) paper, I want you to draw a large circle and divide it into quarters by making a horizontal line and a vertical line. At this point, you can either hold your Medicine Wheel vertically or if you feel inclined, you could hold it where the top of the Medicine Wheel has a V shape. It is up to you and either orientation is fine. You are going to take a shamanic journey looking for any information regarding the direction of the East. I could give you a page of information of things that are often associated with the direction of the East, or you could also Google it, and if you did either one, you would be the negating the very skill I'm about to teach you. I want to remind you that across all time and cultures there have been people who could get information that was not written or given to them from other people. It is actually *these people* who kept the tribe or community safe and healthy. If we only get our information from the internet, what good will we do ourselves if we should ever not have access to information this way, or if it is incorrect information.

The information that we can get from being in heightened states of awareness is coded, so to speak, for us individually. I want to stress, forget what you think you may know about the four directions, and certainly do not look it up anywhere else, for you are going to learn how to get this information in a new way.

When you take your shamanic journey to the East, which will be your first journey, I want you to see if you can get a sense of what color is in *your* direction of the East. See if you can find a bird associated with that direction, also an animal in that direction, a season, and also an element. (Air, Water, Earth and Fire)

If at first you don't get all this information, do not worry about it. Get what you can and draw and write it inside your Medicine Wheel. If for example you see the color yellow in the East, then color your medicine wheel in that quadrant yellow with color pencils and draw the bird or animals that you see. You can write in information as well. You will continue to do this with each of the remaining directions.

The next one being the South. Look for the same information, followed by the West and lastly, the North.

Unless you are *very skilled and practiced* at shamanic journeying it is not recommended to do four journeys in a row. It is much better to let a day or two pass between each journey. You may find yourself getting better at this by the time you reach the North, since at that point, you will have done it three times prior. You can always do another journey to gather more information for any direction you feel you may not have enough information for. You want your Medicine Wheel to be chock-full of information.

This speaks more to our lack of non-linear education in the modern western culture than anything else. We have to get in a heightened state of awareness to find out what the direction East means to us and our heart or the direction West or the other two directions!

41

Generations ago, our ancestors had relationships with the directions and understood what they meant. But we are in a state of evolution where we have to remember things we have long forgotten. The more information you have on your Medicine Wheel, the easier it will be for you to progress with the rest of the divination systems. You're also exploring how you see the world and your place in it, by having an understanding of the directions, the seasons, the times of day, the birds, the animals and the elements. All these things are sentient, but that's another book.

Once your Medicine Wheel is done, (*Congratulations!*) you're ready for the next

42

step. Of course you could always add to your Medicine Wheel as time and years go by, and I would expect you to do so as your awareness also grows over time.

I say, *'I hold my Medicine Wheel within me.'* I have a strong relationship with the information in my Wheel and can remember it easily without the added help of a visual reminder. Some day you will too. Until then, happily use the Wheel you are creating.

Divination Systems

The divination systems that we will be covering are Tarot, I Ching, Bibliomancy, Tea

43

Leaf Reading, the Pendulum, Reading Rocks and Reading Sticks.

I have found that each of these divination systems have their own gift. For example, with Tarot, it is very helpful to determine **which path** would be in our best interest and I will show you a card layout that is my favorite for this. With the I Ching, comes the gift of knowing the **best process** to accomplish the goal. With bibliomancy, we received immediate inspiration. We can get immediate clarity with a pendulum. The Reading of rocks and sticks is beneficial for seeing what is Seen in the situation, and what Unseen Forces are affecting a situation. You could use all of these

44

systems for one question, or one or two, depending on what you feel like doing. For me personally, if I have a big decision I am contemplating I will do a Tarot Reading to see which direction to go, and often times it can be startlingly clear with the Tarot. And then, I follow it up with an I Ching Reading, to see what is the best process for me to take to accomplish my goal.

Chapter Three

TAROT

"Life is not a matter of holding good cards, but of playing a poor hand well."
Robert Louis Stevenson

Tarot Card Reading is an old divination

system and is

beloved by

many for very

good reason.

I know some

exceptional

Tarot

Divination with playing cards is recorded as early as 1540.

A manuscript from 1750 (Pratesi Cartomancer) documents rudimentary divinatory meanings for the cards. In 1765, Casanova wrote in his diary that his Russian mistress frequently used a deck of cards for divination. I can already guess what she was looking for with the cards.

Readers, but what I am teaching you today, you don't need to have any background in Tarot. Indeed, I am teaching you how to see things differently. So I would like you to get your Tarot deck, preferably the Rider-Waite deck, or something similar to that. You could work with an oracle or angel deck or something similar if you want later on. But for clarity, The Rider Waite deck (or something similar, you want a deck that has the Major Arcana, Minor Arcana, and Court Cards) is optimal for this exercise.

I want you to take the deck and divide it into thirds. One third will be the Major Arcana cards of which there are 22 and include images like the Sun, the Lovers, Death, etc.

Then take the rest of the cards and divide them into a stack of the Court cards, and that would include the Ace, King, Queen, Jack in all the suits. Which leaves you with the remainder being Minor Arcana cards, which would be the cards in all suits starting with the two and going through to the ten. Once you have these cards divided this way, get your journal and be prepared to take notes.

First, craft your question. And remember that the question is the most important part of the Reading. The better the question, the clearer the answer.

This card layout is best suited for decisions that are A or B. For example, if you are trying to determine if a career change is in your best interest at this current time in your life, and if it's for your highest and best good, (notice how I am framing the question), you are going to have choice between A and B. You can also ask this card layout what your life would look like staying in your current relationship and also what it would look like leaving your current relationship, if that is something that you are questioning. Anything that has the two choices is perfect for this layout. So I want you to get in a calm state of mind, with clarity as your intention. Certainly start with a prayer that will sound something like this: *'I asked for clear and unobstructed guidance from my higher self and my Guardians regarding my decision of ...'*

Then with each of the three decks laid out in front of you, hold your clear question in your mind. (If you don't have your question in a clear concise way, and is instead a couple of sentences, then stop, until you can have the question down to just one sentence possibly two. One is preferred.) Make your question completely clear with no wishy-washiness and **never use the word should.** Whenever we use the word should in a Reading the answer will almost always be yes, because again, in the great Universe there's room and space for every possibility. It is also dis-empowering to use the word *should* in any inquiry to your life. So be extra vigilant that you don't use that word in your question and take a few minutes to craft the perfect question.

Presently, you have your very precise question and your three decks shuffled and neatly arranged in front of you. I want you to pick one card from the Court cards and place it in front of you on your left. Then pick another Court card and place it in front of you on your right. It should also be said at this point the left side will be the answer to your question if you

52

say stay in your current job and the right side
will be what it looks like if you change your
career. It doesn't matter which side you put this
on. All that matters is that you have the
intention that the left side is designated for one
outcome and the right side will be designated
for the alternative outcome. Keep the cards
face down at this point. Then pick three cards
from the Minor Arcana stack, and place them
three on the left and three more on the right.

Each side of the three cards sits directly
underneath the Court card and again face
down. Then pick one card from the Major
Arcana and place that above both the layouts.

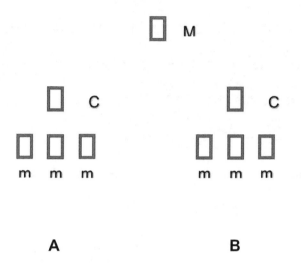

A   B

M = Major Arcana

C = Court Card

M = Minor Arcana

 Right now you should have two card layouts one to your left, one to your right, with one card vertically above both. Before you turn the cards over make sure you're completely clear which

54

side is going to be the current situation or similar, and what side is going to be if you take A or B path.

Now spend a moment looking at them. *Soften your gaze so you are not looking at them hard.*

Sometimes the difference in tone between the two sides is significant and obvious. I find this to be true most of the time. If you have an understanding of how to read Tarot you can use those skills as well, but I want you to adjust your site to see what the overall tone is what you're looking at. You're going to be looking for any significant numbers of one particular suit or if there are cards that appear more challenging on one side than the other side. The Court card that sits above the row of three, represents you in this situation. The Court card represents you if you decide to take a certain path on the left and the other Court card represents you if you take the alternative path on the right. Spend a few minutes looking at these two individuals and see which one you would rather be or aspire to. Do not look up a meaning of a card if you are already not familiar with it. You will delay learning how to do this if you do. Don't reach outside yourself but go within.

Which of the Court cards do you prefer? Okay, to gain more clarity look at the three

56

cards underneath each of the Court cards. The one on the left represents the past, the center one represents now, and the one on the right represents the future. Of course, remember the future is not written in stone and changes whenever we make a significant change in our intention or life. In the case of the alternative choice you might ask how can one of the bottom Minor Arcana cards represent the past when I haven't done that proposed idea yet. If that is the case, then you're going to want to look at that card more as what has been building in your life that has brought you to the place where you are even contemplating this other choice. That would represent the past. The card in the middle that represents the now would be what your life would look like right now taking either paths, and the future card represents the likely outcome. I think in many ways the future card is the most significant. If the future card does not look like something I want in my life, then I will refer back to the past card to see if the reason why the future is not going to work out the way I wanted to is because of how I have been in my past. And if that is the case, then I will change my behavior or life to make it more amenable towards a brighter future. This is why Tarot can be an amazing tool for self-reflection. It can also be brutally honest.

At this point it might be very clear which is the most beneficial path for you to take but there is still one more critical thing to look at and that is a Major Arcana card that is sitting over both storylines. You do not have to have any background in Tarot to see that if you have the Sun card, it is pointing to abundant blessings and all manner of good thing. If you have the Death card, that could be sobering for some people to see, but we also know it could represent the end of something old so that something new can be born. I can think of a number of things in life, that would be more beneficial if they would come to an end. It's hard to birth something new unless we let go of something old. Reading the Trump card, look at the images and relax your eyes and allow your imagination to step into the card. Imagine you are living in the time of the card and you are having a dialogue with this Major Arcana (or also known as a trump) card. This is when it's beneficial that you have taken shamanic journeys because it won't be that big a stretch to imagine yourself doing this. You've already loosened up some of your overly rigid left brain thinking.

*See what the trump card can tell you because it is the **overseeing, archetypal lesson** on either choice. This is also helpful for us to have a deeper understanding of what motivates us and the trump card will say, in* *part, what that is.* It is the card that's telling us what we need to learn by the lesson presented. If we have a deep understanding of that, we can maybe bypass any troublesome lesson.

I often recommend at this point that people take a picture of the card layouts with their cell phone. I think it's helpful to look at the card layout over the next few days while you are determining what your best road to progress is. And if there is any temptation toward wavering, like often there is if it's an entirely new path, the visual reminder of the card layout can help inspire us to stay the course. This leads us to the next divination system: the ancient *I Ching*.

Chapter Four

I CHING

There is a time for being ahead,
a time for being behind;
a time for being in motion,
a time for being at rest;
a time for being vigorous,
a time for being exhausted;
a time for being safe,
a time for being in danger.
Lao Tzu, Tao Te Ching

It could be said that the *I Ching*

(pronounced E Ching) is the most scholarly

divination system and certainly one of the

oldest. It is also called *The Book of Changes,*

also sometimes called *The Laws of Change.*

(We work with translations handed down

through time, just as we do with the works of the great Rumi and others.)

The *I Ching* was inspired by Fu Hsi during the third millennium B.C. He 'discovered' (better put 'was inspired') the eight trigrams and followed this up with the sixty-four hexagrams. But it was through the development of King Wen's efforts, as he sat incarcerated and beheld a vision on the wall of his cell, that gave inspired life and fuller written meanings for each of the sixty-four hexagrams. (He later was able to take his throne again)

The Great Confucius found the *I Ching* so powerful he wished he had another fifty years to live so that he might better study and understand this to 'avoid great error in his life and become without fault.'

In more recent times, Carl Jung saw the enormous benefit of this divination system. He sought and secured funds to have an American version published.

Why? Because it is uncannily accurate.

It is interesting to note too; some people have attributed the *I Ching* as the foundational source for Feng Shui. Their similarities cannot be over looked.

I am challenged to find a way to describe, in greater detail, of how the *I Ching* is laid out, without it becoming too much information, that might put some of you off. This is not a cop-out, but really, how can I describe how it is connected to the elements, yin and yang, and natural features of the landscape etc. without it requiring a lengthy chapter at best. Or worse, you come away with the thought, it has no application as a divination system for you and is too much effort. I am avoiding this possibility by offering almost nothing in the way of further description, but be assured, as you practice this, your understanding will grow. And it will grow fast!

Though intelligent and thoughtful people have made a lifetime study of the *I Ching,* that is not how we are to understand it, because we are taking a crash course, but my hope is that you might explore it deeper on your own, over time.

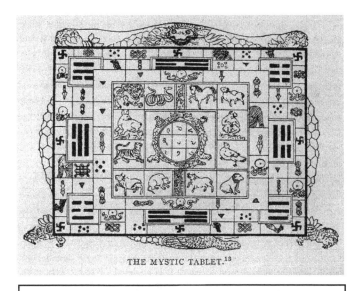

THE MYSTIC TABLET.[15]

The Mystic Tablet from ancient China depicting the I Ching on the back of a tortoise.

To best see how the *I Ching* can work as a method of a divination, I want you to take your question that you posed to the Tarot deck and now pose it to the *I Ching*. This gives you the added benefit of seeing how the two different systems, respond to the same question.

Take the choice (path A or B) that you decided upon during your Tarot Reading.

Whichever path you determine was in your best interest, now ask the *I Ching* **how you can best accomplish your goal.**

And as with everything, when we go to the spirit world it's best to start with a prayer. It's more for our protection than anything else. So you can start again with the prayer, that I mentioned above, which goes something like *'I seek clear, unobstructed guidance from my higher self and my guardian(s) for what is in my best interest regarding the situation of ...'*

For the *I Ching* you can purchase official *I Ching* coins. My preferred method is to take one quarter, one dime, and one nickel and use them as my coins that will be tossed in the Reading. You're going to want to have your trusty journal nearby to write down your intention or question. I recommend dating this entry.

With the three coins in your hand, gently shake them and toss them in front of you, holding your question in your mind. You will do this six times, writing in your journal the pattern from these. The first toss will be your bottom line, the second toss line sits right above the first, the third toss lines sits above the second and, so on. It will look something like this:

```
_____   _____   ●
_____
_____   _____
_____  ●
_____
_____
```

The above configuration would be coin tosses of this order: (*bottom to top*)

1. Two heads, one tail

2. Two heads, one tail

3. Three heads (hence the dot)

4. Two tails, one head

5. Two heads, one tail

6. Three tails (hence the dot)

Each combination has its own line pattern:

Three heads = a solid line, followed by a dot.

Two heads and one tail = a solid line.

Three tails = a broken line followed by a dot.

Two tails and one head = a broken line.

Dots indicate movement, and hence form a new hexagram. The above hexagram is followed by a new one that looks like this:

```
——————————————
——————————————
————  ————
————  ————
——————————————
——————————————
```

The dot signifies movement and the line is considered a *moving line*. A moving line reverts to its' opposite. For example, if you have a broken line followed by a dot, then it becomes a solid line.

Does this all sound confusing? Once you have done this a couple of times, you will see how easy it is to do.

In the examples of the two hexagrams above the first is # 5 and is titled **Calculated Waiting**, (Perseverance *brings good fortune for the Superior Person. The reference to the 'Superior Person' is when one is acting and thinking from their best perspective*) and it transforms into # 61 titled **Insight. (***The Superior Person gives thought to justice before execution)*

Both explanations for the hexagrams here are small snippets, as the full hexagrams are very detailed. You would then read the accompanying text which will show the tendencies of what is to come, plus even more helpful, the best course of action. It would be very hard for a novice to memorize all sixty-four hexagrams initially, so this is where you can read the meanings through a plethora of books available. My preferred booked for the *I Ching* is the ***I Ching Workbook* by R.L. Wing.** He goes into greater detail then I am right now and I have found it enormously helpful and have recommended it to everyone taking this course over the years. For a more scholarly and detailed opportunity, I prefer ***The Laws of Change I Ching and the Philosophy of Life* by Jack M. Balkin.**   I often work with both

74

books when I'm doing an *I Ching* Reading. I also enjoy **The I Ching; Perfect Companion by Gary Melyan.**

This is your hexagram and this is your answer as amazing as that sounds.

As you will come to find through a little research, the broken lines represent Yin energy and the solid lines represent Yang energy not unlike the left and right side of your brain. If you throw a hexagram that is all yin energy, it's pointing to an imbalance. A same imbalance is when it is all yang in a hexagram. The order of the yin and yang lines are also very telling. If you have a yang base, with no

moving lines, it can point to great stability or
stubbornness depending on the position of the
rest of the lines. As I already mentioned, each
of the hexagrams are also connected with the
elements (Fire, Water, Air and Earth) as well
as features in the landscape (Mountain, Lake,
Thunder, Heaven). This is where R.L. Wings *I
Ching Workbook* comes in handy. There is
information online as well about the different
hexagrams which could be worthwhile reading.
The *I Ching* is also about progression from the
first hexagram to the completion of a journey
ending with the 64th hexagram. This is in
common with the Tarot deck which starts with
the Fool in the major arcana, and ends with
The World card. The Tarot is sometimes called

the Fools Journey and we can see our part, in that great archetypal procession, when we use the Tarot for self-reflection.

I always find it inspiring when I get the Fool, or the first hexagram in the *I Ching*, because it's telling me I can help direct the birth of this project or situation. Nothing is written in stone and I have greater flexibility working with the beginning of something then the middle of something. If I do a Reading for myself and I'm not happy with what the outcome is, I spend the time needed to see what I need to change in my life to make it a better outcome and then this way divination is a tool to success and not a fortune-telling instrument. I also will sometimes do another Reading for more clarity or validation of the previous Reading.

You may find the *I Ching* fascinating enough that you even study its brainchild *Feng Shui* and you will have a deeper understanding of that system of balance by having some background and knowledge of the *I Ching.*

Chapter Five

PENDULUM (AND MORE)

"Also, go inside and listen to your body, because your body will never lie to you. Your mind will play tricks, but the way you feel in your heart, in your guts, is the truth."
Miguel Ruiz

Let's move on now to a little bit of an easier method of divination and that is the age-old use of the pendulum. The pendulum is simply anything that is suspended from a chain (or something similar) and that can be swung over the hand or the body to gain (primarily) yes and no answers. As far as divination systems go, I find this one the most pesky. I have found it to be inaccurate and thus I have a tendency to give my results a sidewise glance. I have come to understand it gives me the answer *that is best for me at that time*…which is not always the truth. I think it can be helpful, used daily, to develop a quick and intuitive way to get information fast.

Gut Feeling

If one gets really good at the pendulum, you could eliminate it entirely and just use your gut feeling or body. It is basically the same and our gut feelings are always ready to go. I have taught many teens the skill of Reading their gut. We start by picking an obvious yes answer and saying aloud, (for me), *"I love sunny days in May!"* I feel what that feels like in my stomach. I then say aloud an obvious no, for me: "*I love being frozen to the point of pain."* There is a difference of sensation in the stomach, though usually subtle at first. With abundant practice comes a highly developed and dependable skill. You can easily use this when speaking with someone to determine if they are telling the truth and more. Plus, you don't have to say, "*Wait a second while I whip out my pendulum!"*

Pendulum

You will want to determine what the swing direction is for you with a pendulum that equates to a yes answer, and the swing direction that equates to a no answer. I have a small amethyst that is cut in a diamond shape that hangs from a delicate chain that I have used for twenty years that I use as my pendulum. I keep it in a small velvet bag in my purse at all times. I often call it 'my rock', and when I need a quick yes or no answer I check with 'my rock'.

I have come to find though if I am too emotionally invested in the outcome of a yes or no answer, I have a hard time getting out of my own way for clarity. And that is when I go to my rock aka pendulum.

Muscle Testing

82

It is not unlike muscle testing for information as well. Another name for this is **Kinesiology.** It is a simple method for monitoring and assessing mental, emotional, and physical states.

One method is to hold your ring finger to your thumb. Ask a few definite yes answers and a few definite no answers, while trying to break the bond with your right hand pointer finger. If it breaks through easily it is a 'no'. If there is resistance, it is a 'yes'. You could also ask if a food is good for you this way or another method would be by holding the food in question in front of you and drawing it from your head down to your stomach and if you feel pulled forward it's a 'yes' and if there is no movement, then a 'no'. This feeling is almost magnetic in sensation. There are some well-respected health practitioners in the holistic field that use this method to validate what they believe is the best remedy for a client. It is the 'cousin' of the pendulum in my opinion.

But to get back to the pendulum, you will want to acquire one that you feel drawn to or one that you would not mind looking at for years to come. You could also make one by using any pointed object *(although it should be noted I have seen some beautiful round crystal spheres, about the size of a marble, that are also used for pendulum work and work just as well as one with a pointed tip*), and attach it to something like a necklace chain or something similar. Much like anything else, you can do the simple method of pendulum work like I'm describing or you can really take this to a deeper level and use it for dowsing, as it's also called, for most almost anything.

Dowsers are the ones who can find water when no machine can. According to Wikipedia:

*Dowsing is also known as **divining, doodle bugging** (particularly in the United States, in searching for petroleum) or (when searching specifically for water) **water finding, water*** *witching (in the United States) or **water dowsing**.*

Unlike Wikipedia, who claims there is no proof dowsing works, I *know* it works. When I lived in Mystic, CT and had a well that ran dry, no one was able to locate more water on our land. We were in a bit of a panic. I found a local dowser to come to our home and he found water within minutes and they dug (pretty deep!) and there was a glorious amount of water that we were able to access and that well never ran dry again!

Dowsers can also work with the **ley lines** (energy grid lines) of the Earth too which is a fascinating subject. The ley lines can have an enormous effect on our health, and we would do well to have more people working in this field.

This course is more of a psychic sampler so that you can see what resonates with you and what you feel gives you the best results and then if you want to explore any of these divination systems, then by all means, I encourage you to do so!

Take your pendulum, and hold it in your dominant hand over the palm of your non dominant hand. I hold my left palm up and hold the end of my pendulum chain about one foot above my palm. Of course I start with a prayer before I ask any question. I also take a moment or two to make sure my question is about me and not somebody else's life per se, so that I am ethical in my inquiry.

I then make an obvious 'yes' statement, which for me is usually *'today is… (I say the day of the week) and the weather is… (and I say what the weather is.)* Simple. My 'yes' response is the pendulum swinging away from me and back towards me. Some days its' swing is wider than other days. I note that, then I will know what to expect with regards to the amount of swing, from the response of the pendulum to my inquiry. (somedays it is just a small swing, other days a very wide swing) I then make an obvious 'no' statement which is usually, '*I see before my eyes a herd of elephants.*' The pendulum then swings left to right. It is 'set' at that point and 'good to go' for my divination. I then ask my question or questions, and when finished, place it back it its drawstring bag. If later in the day I want to use the pendulum again I always start with a prayer and then I also state the obvious 'yes' and 'no' statements to reset my pendulum.

If it swings in a circle to the right instead of a definite back and forth that's telling me a probable 'yes'. If it swings more to the left but still in a circular way, that means it's a probable 'no'. It could also mean that there are other things I need to understand that are not part of my inquiries at that moment. If this sounds complicated, it is not in practice, I can assure you. I have seen some people whose 'yes' and 'no' direction of swing are the opposite of mine, to which I say if that's the way your pendulum works for you, then so be it! It's better to determine what is a 'yes' and what it is a 'no' response from your pendulum then how it is for me.

Once, I saw a woman pull out her pendulum at a discount clothing store in front of a large shoe rack, and I laughed to myself as I thought what a funny way to use a pendulum! To decide whether or not to get a particular pair of shoes!

Chakras

Another level of pendulum work is with the chakras. It is very helpful for determining the health of the chakras at *that time*. Our chakras are not static and can change during the course of the day. Each chakra corresponds to many things about us

> These swirling wheels of energy correspond to massive nerve centers in the body. Each of the seven main chakras contains bundles of nerves and major organs as well as our psychological, emotional, and spiritual states of being. Since everything is moving, it's essential that our seven main chakras stay open, aligned, and fluid.
> *Deepak Chopra*

and it is best to research this independently, as this book is not focusing on that information.

Hold the pendulum over your (hard to do your own, but try it on a friend) chakras to see the health of them. (*you could do your own chakras by drawing an outline of your body on an 8" x 11" piece of paper and using the pendulum over the areas that represent your chakras.*) That could be an eye-opening experience. If the chakras are too big it shows fear, amongst other possible reasons. If the chakras are too small, it can point to an unhealthy shutting down. Many women have an undersized throat chakra which is the chakra of communication and expression of feelings. If the chakras are all mismatched sizes, it shows the energetic system is not balanced at all. Through conscious awareness, and *intentional imagination*, we can bring them back into balance. It is a great tool also for healers that are working with clients, to check their clients chakras, which are filled with an enormous amount of information. If the heart chakra is too open, the person will feel overwhelmed with empathy for everyone. If the third eye chakra is too open, there will be too much psychic information flooding in. An enlarged root chakra shows a strong fear of basic needs (like food and shelter) not being met, and so on.

The pendulum can also be used to help find things that are lost, by walking into the room where you believe you may have left something, and seeing the pendulum respond as you walk around; big circles mean 'yes'. It is much like the game played when we were young: Hotter and Colder. (*your getting hotter!, as you get closer to the goal*)

Chapter Six

BIBLIOMANCY

"You can never get a cup of tea large enough or a book long enough to suit me."
C.S. Lewis

Bibliomancy is the ability to get information from a book. It is a wonderfully fun way to get information and validation from a source outside of oneself.

All you need to do is:

- Say your prayer,

- Clarify your question,

- Pull a book off the shelf.

You can pick a random book or you could pick a book intentionally. It is best to set the intention of how many sentences you will read to get your answer.

When I initially did this, if I didn't like what my fingers had landed on for an answer, I would keep reading until I found sentences that were more to my liking. I realized the folly of my behavior. So at this point, I limit myself to three sentences and however tempted I am to keep reading, I discipline myself to stop at three.

You decide ahead of time before you open the book, how many sentences *you* will use for your Oracle reading. Then open the book and let the pages' flip slowly back and forth and without letting your eyes fall on any particular page. Then let your finger point directly down on a page in the book. That is the first sentence and then read on to how many sentences your prior agreement was. This is also a remarkable way to get either validation or inspiration for a question that may have been burning in your heart for a while. It's also very much like reading a Chinese fortune cookie in that you may have to see the metaphor in the meaning and how it applies to your question. I also, always ask a question before I read a fortune cookie!

After twenty plus years of doing Dreamwork, it is very easy for me to look at things metaphorically and it is my preferred way of working most of the time. This is one of the benefits of looking with new eyes; the ability to find the metaphor or symbolic meaning of something. I know a few people that find bibliomancy their preferred method of divination and they have found great success with this simple and easy method.

Chapter Seven

TEA LEAF READING

"Tea is an act complete in its simplicity.
When I drink tea, there is only me and the tea.
The rest of the world dissolves.
There are no worries about the future.
No dwelling on past mistakes.
Thich Nhat Hanh

Do you want to know how to be a good Tea

Leaf Reader? If you can read clouds you can

read tea leaves and vice versa. The skill is

softening your eyesight and moving to the right

side of your brain where your imagination

reigns supreme and you can easily see

images. My great-grandmother was a Tea Leaf

Reader (and made money at it) during the Great Depression. So when a friend who organizes psychic fairs, asked me if I would be willing to do Tea Leaf Readings one day, I gladly agreed as a way of honoring my great-grandmother Helen Dufort. I found it very easy. So much so, that I would show the person that I was 'reading' for also how to do it. They got a quick mini lesson in a fifteen-minute Reading. I guess I am a teacher at heart.

Tasseography is the official name of Tea Leaf Reading and also encompasses Reading Coffee grinds. In the Victorian era, it was practiced as an art and also as a means to while away the afternoon hours. It is filled with ritualistic behavior developed in the Victorian

era and included things like taking the spoon

and swirling it three times to the left and one

time to the right etc. and all this extra behavior

which at first I

used to look

at as just

distractions. I

am now

inclined to

> Traveling gypsies, as the Roma people were then known, had long taken up the practice of tea-leaf readings, often going door-to-door to offer their services. By the mid-1800s, the Roma had become part of the social scene, welcomed into both parlors and tea rooms to give readings for a fee.
>
> *Laurel Dalrympal*

look at it in a new light. It may very well be that

it took that amount of distractive ritual to get

the people involved in the Reading to get into a

different mindset. All that focused intention on

holding the cup a certain way etc. would start

to shift their awareness so that they could
Read the leaves easier.

But when I read Tea Leaves, I don't take
that much time and I usually try to do it within
fifteen minutes so I get down to business pretty
quick. I use loose leaf tea that I have pre-made
and stored in a mason jar. I have about a
dozen different antique teacups that I bring and
I have the client pick their cup and saucer. The
tea cup does not have to match the saucer I let
them know. Even as they pick the cup, I am
gathering information because each teacup
has its own personality and images on it so I
start the Reading right off the bat.

And because I like to Read, I will Read the saucer as well as the cup, and I'll tell you that in a little bit.

Here is the process:

- I have them take about a teaspoon of the loose leaf tea (which is now a soupy watery mix) and place it in the bottom of the tea cup. Oops, I almost forgot I start with a prayer first and ask them to present **one** question. (Tea Leaf Readings are best done with one question)

- I have them place the tea in the cup with just a little bit of the tea mixture. Again, in a more formal and longer version of this, the client would drink the cup of tea contemplating their question and go from there.

- I have them swirl the cup three times to the right

- Take the saucer and invert it on top of the cup.

- Tap the saucer once with their spoon.

- Hold the saucer to the cup *firmly* and turn the whole kit and caboodle over in one fell swoop.

- Lift the cup off the saucer and place it to the side of the saucer.

This leaves tea leaves clinging to the sides of the cup that I will read. But first I look at the saucer and I look for any type of a pattern in the soupy mixture on it. Sometimes there are noticeable images, sometimes not very much. I then Read the cup and hold the cup so that the handle is *facing my heart* and the handle represents the client. I divide the cup, in my mind, into quarters. I 'see' a visible horizontal and vertical line. Everything below the horizontal line is what is unseen to the client which can include ancestral tendencies, and also closest to their heart. Everything

105

above the horizontal line is that which is seen and known, and also help from the Spiritual World. To the left of the vertical line is the past and also represents the feminine. To the right of the vertical line, is the future and can also represent the masculine. If there are tea leaves that are crossing any of these Nexus points it shows more significant movement then if it was just sitting squarely in one of the quadrants. So if it shows me there's movement from the past to the future, and if most of it is above the horizon line, this shows a situation that is easily understood by the client. Not so if most of it is below the horizon line. All kinds of other details can be finessed out of layout. I then look at the tea leaves in much the same way

106

as Reading a cloud, in that I am looking for images to pop out at me. I get my eyes and my sight *very soft*, and with very little imagination, I can see different images and then put those images in the context of where they are sitting in the cup or time frame. From this information I'm able to put it together a Reading.

At this point, I usually take a pencil and point to the different images I'm seeing in the cup, as well as their relevant location, to show the client what I am seeing. They always respond with surprise when they can see exactly what I am when I point it out. It's interesting to think about the days of old when a gypsy woman would hold the cup, move it around a little bit and say nothing with the

silent suspense building all around her. And

then, in a theatrical way, share the information

of what she saw. I think this could also be

enjoyable but I would rather teach people how

to do it, then to come across as the Great

Gypsy Woman Fortune Teller.

Chapter Eight

READING ROCKS

*"Do not be afraid; our fate
cannot be taken from us; it is a gift."* Dante Alighieri, Inferno

We are moving right along to the segment
where I teach you how to Read Rocks. This is
different than holding a gemstone in your hand
and getting information, which is also a
legitimate way to communicate with a rock. My
method is more like the Tea Leaf Reading

though. And this is where you will put to good use your Medicine Wheel.

But first you will need to determine how many rocks you would like to Read. The best way to do this is to pick your **favorite number**. You certainly want at least three rocks and anything more than nine becomes a little unruly. It is up to you the number you pick. All this gives us an opportunity to also develop a deepening relationship with numbers. What does the number one, number two, the number three and so on mean to you? If you don't have much of a response, as I'm asking you these questions, then it's a good time now to come up with meaning for the different numbers. And don't go looking on the Internet or to outside sources for information. At least not at this point! I would like you to pick up your journal and write the number one equals.... and give it some attributes. For me it would be Beginnings, Independence, Inclusiveness, Fire, January and more. I want you to do this with each of the numbers from one to ten or you could even go thirteen. Eleven, twelve and thirteen are powerhouse numbers. If you are struggling to attach meaning to any of the numbers, do not worry about it, go to the next number. You can go back to those numbers that need more attributes later. I recommend taking a shamanic journey to the specific numbers you feel no connection with and develop a deeper understanding of what they might be.

Once you have a better idea of what the numbers mean to you, pick the number that you want to use for rock divination work. Then go and pick the rocks that you will use for this.

When I work with groups, I usually have them go outside and pick up small stones. But you could also use gemstones or tumbled stones if that's what you prefer. As you pick your rocks' I want you to have in mind what rock is going to represent a 'yes' answer, what rock is going to represent a 'no' answer, what rock is going to represent a 'heart based' solution, what rock is going to represent a 'maybe', what rock is going to represent a 'thinking based' solution and you might come up with some more meanings you want to attach to the rocks. Just keep in mind you're going to have to keep track of all of this in your memory.

For me I usually pick a white rock for 'yes', black rock for a 'no', a rose-colored rock for the 'heart based' solution, a blue colored rock for the 'thinking' solution, a green rock for healing solutions.   This can be an enormous amount of fun. Then I want you to write out and draw a 'key' in your journal for the rock and its' meaning.   (The key is a chart showing which

113

rock has which attribute) Don't worry if you don't feel like you can't draw well enough. This is only for your eyes and you can certainly do a good enough job to make it a useful key.

Now you can get your Medicine Wheel and lay it in front of you either on the floor or on the table. I prefer the floor because when I drop the rocks onto the Medicine Wheel I think they land better, if they are landing on the floor as opposed to furniture.

You can now say your prayer and state clearly your inquiry, then gently drop your rocks over the Medicine Wheel.

The first moment or two looking at your Medicine Wheel with rocks randomly all over it, may seem impossible to determine any information. But if you *soften your eyes* and let the images and their meanings reveal themselves, you can get a remarkable amount of information. For instance, if any of the rocks are outside the circle you want to ask yourself what does that mean? It might mean that it is irrelevant to the question. If the 'thinking rock' is below the horizon line, it means sub conscious thoughts. If it is above the horizon line, it's that's what is seen, known and conscious thinking. If it is to the left of the vertical line, it is from the past or from the feminine depending on the context of the

115

question. If it is on the right side it is going towards the future or the masculine depending on the question. And now you have all the other wonderful details in your Medicine Wheel including seasons, times of day, colors, elements, attributes of power animals etc. Your Medicine Wheel is a wealth of information.

The rocks that you have thrown have their own information that you have attributed to them. You can now give a *very full Reading* this way. To the average person walking by, they would never have any idea what Reading would be attached to a bunch of rocks on a colorful circle, sitting on the floor. But to you, with your adjusted sight, it is a mini story before your eyes.

116

Chapter Nine

READING STICKS

"There is a vitality, a life force, an energy, a quickening that is translated through you into action, and because there is only one of you in all of time, this expression is unique."
Martha Graham

Reading Sticks is very much like Reading Rocks. You're going to pick a number that you want to work with, which could be the same number as the number you picked for the rocks. You are going to go outside and get that amount of sticks. I recommend getting sticks no more than five inches long or breaking a larger stick into smaller pieces. You don't want them too small either. You can also finish this with picking sticks from *different trees* or from *your favorite tree*. I often use birch sticks when I read this way. If you would like to use multiple species of trees, hopefully you have an understanding and relationship with the different species, and if not, then you can shamanically journey to learn more about the trees. A birch tree is often associated with beginnings as it is one of the first trees to grow after a fire. An oak tree often represents strength since it is one the hardest woods. A maple tree can represent usefulness and utility since every part of the tree is used, including

118

its sap for sweet maple syrup. A pine tree can represent looking from a higher perspective and well as a vulnerability since they are easily broken in high wind. This is fun and enriching to identify with Nature in methods like this. I think it would be worthwhile to explore this deeper and it would certainly enhance your Reading as well.

I also recommend one straight stick for a 'yes' answer, a curved stick for a 'no', a wiggly stick or forked stick for a 'maybe', and so on.

You will then take your bundle of sticks and, standing over your Medicine Wheel, say your prayer aloud and your question of inquiry and drop the sticks on your Medicine Wheel. You will read them in the same manner as you did with the rocks. Again, anyone walking by would never guess what you were doing and yet the visual images will be very clear to you within a few minutes.

I know back in the old fashioned days when it was considered dangerous to do this kind of work (could be looked at as witchcraft), people would draw a circle in the sand or even an imaginary circle with their mind and throw the sticks or the rocks or whatever they had and Read that way. If you know your Medicine Wheel very well, you carry it with inside your heart and you don't need the physical Medicine Wheel on paper in front of you. But until you're able to do that on your own, without any struggle, then you use the one you have created in front of you.

Chapter Ten

AUGURY

"I am a cage, in search of a bird."

Franz Kafka

Augury is the ability to Read the flight of birds in the sky. You can look to traditional meanings for the birds but why not come up with your own? Look up at the sky and draw a large imaginary circle and quarter it much like your Medicine Wheel.

Say your prayer and ask your clear question
of intent and see what birds fly into your great
circle. What direction are they are going and
take your Medicine Wheel (in your mind) and
place it in the great sky above you. If you can
attach meaning to the individual birds that you
see, all the better!

Are you sensing how you can do this
anywhere and with almost anything? Because
you *are able* to do so. If you are able to Read
one of these well, you can Read anything in
the same fashion.

Of course it's like anything else, the more
you practice, the better you get. The advantage

of doing this in a workshop with other people is you can see firsthand how their Readings are so clear and obvious. Sometimes it's easier to read somebody else than ourselves. So why not practice and have fun with somebody else Reading Sticks for them or Rocks, or *anything else* that your heart desires!

Index

About the Author

Susan Morgan

Susan Morgan is the Founder of **The Mystic Dream Center**, a 501 C non-profit, dedicated to empowerment through Dreamwork. She is also a Spiritual Psychic Medium and Author of numerous books.

Susan lives in New Hampshire and works nationally speaking, leading workshops and helping people gain clarity through her Readings.

More information can be found on:
MysticDreamCenter.com

40394155R00081

Made in the USA
Middletown, DE
11 February 2017